OTHER TITLES FROM AIRLIE PRESS

THE
ANIMAL
AT
YOUR
SIDE

THE
ANIMAL
AT
YOUR
SIDE

MEGAN
ALPERT

Airlie Press
PORTLAND
OREGON
2020

Airlie Press is supported by book sales and grants, by contributions to the press from its supporters, and by the work donated by all the poet-editors of the press.

P.O. Box 68441
Portland OR 97268
www.airliepress.org

email: editors@airliepress.org

Cover Art: "Grafted, Expected to Take" by Sara Everett
Book Design: Beth Ford, Glib Communications & Design
https://bethford.design

First Edition
ISBN: 978-1-950404-05-6
Library of Congress Control Number: 2019957028
Printed in the United States of America

For Mollie, for Myer,
for Ruth, for Harry,
and those who came before

"She had the boy-girl body of a flower, moving once and for all
past the hermetic front door."

-Medbh McGuckian

CONTENTS

I

TRAILS

DAWN

My sister comes home
smelling of dirt she was buried in,
dandelion milk under her nails.

We wash her arms,
scrub her fingers
with stinging soap,
but still she is not clean.

When she finally speaks,
it's *hand me that trowel*
and *I'll bury the seeds*

while upstairs our grandmother
paces the attic.

Will I wake anywhere
besides this house,
or love anyone ever
beyond my sister
with the skinned knees?

I wake again in the garden
crushing stems against my teeth.

WHAT WE KEPT

We kept the war under our tongues
kept it in our hamstrings
in our bones.
We kept the war in our cereal bowls
in our juice
kept it in our first love
standing in the porch light
waiting to be kissed.
We kept it close
in the hems of our shirts
our face cream
kept it in our bad skin.
We kept it in our driveways
sitting quiet in the yard
flying the Bronx River Parkway, 2 a.m.,
kept it in key rings
smashed into tables,
the imprints they left
on our palms.
We kept it door-to-door
moss-green in hinges.
Kept it mean
under our fingernails
forgotten in our socks—

Sometimes we stood at the edge
of a blueberry field, birds lit
by the last of the sun
but under our skin
the whirr-click of the war beginning . . .

THE WOLF THAT NEVER COMES

The wolf would like a wife

All summer buzzed me awake,
the uncontrollable throats

of the daffodils
open in the yard—

The wolf would like to claw

Inert lawns, torpid houses,
no door swung open,

no pane unlatched—

He would like to set her up against the headboard

Petals or stones against my window,
flitting, uncatchable.

And the waiting clawed off me—

He would like to lick

Perhaps a far-off howl, perhaps
closer

three clear notes—

The wolf would like the pink skin tender, he would like to gnarl,
he would like to lick

The dark was soft. It ate
against my skin.

MY AUNT THE ARTIST, THE LIAR

On the path behind the house, we found the teeth,
but no sign of the corresponding jaw—

whatever had been forced down to earth
had been knocked or dragged elsewhere.

My aunt rattled the teeth
in her cupped palm. Sunlight dropped

a dryness in my mouth—
she was not the kind to tell the truth.

A woman, she said, the teeth
were small, like from a woman's mouth,

and she knelt, pulled down to earth,
her fingers nosed the dirt for further proof.

(My aunt's little rented piece of earth,
a house to make her crazy paintings in.)

They weren't animal teeth. I ran my tongue
along the blank spots in my mouth.

She'd try them in her own mouth
at parties, she told me later, cradling my jaw,

Little one, we rent ourselves from earth.

A GUIDE

Must have walked too quickly
or eaten the breadcrumbs dirty—
must have left the path.

(When the thing left for dead rises
and walks, what is the map she leaves?)

The evening news will call the rest of her "the body."
What rises is different:
half-animal, looks out the sides of its eyes.

No,
    she has gone back for her body.
Visit the original scene. Nothing left
but a hollowed-out rut in the leaves.

DEER SKULL

Coyote chased her down.
Deer treed herself well
through upstate New York—
she was equal to it.
The fire coming out
her eye-holes, nose-holes?
The orange that glows
when the woods are gone.

Reporting From Oil Block 16

We rode to the oil camp in the back of a pickup
on the road that had scared away the animals.
He said his story on the electric company
had been pulled, and we talked corruption. "De hecho,"
he said, "I was a pastor. A year ago my wife
me engañó y no pude seguir. Mi corazón . . ."
(in Spanish, you can say this to a stranger),
"¿No se siente bien?" I finally tried. "No," he smiled,
looking down, "no, it doesn't feel good." My back hurt
from the weight of the tape recorder, the air
of the forest lit us up: wells and pipelines hidden
behind trees whose names and uses we did not know.

IN WOLF COUNTRY

I give you what the wolves left:
a tooth on a leather strap, a few stray
hairs I found stuck to a tree, skull
of a deer the dogs found and licked clean.

Wild dogs, you say, coyotes,
not wolves. You want to transition
without symbols. I trace the sickle scars
where your breasts were, where no one

has ever touched you yet.
They shine in the moonlight—streetlight—
through the window. Later, I thumb
the hairs on your razor and press

my cheek to the rough place
they came from. Sorry, you say, I'll shave
again, and I watch through the mirror
as you file the points down from your teeth.

UNSETTLED

My friend and I went to the lake, found a skull
and took it home. Washed it, set it out to dry
on the shed roof in the sun. Still my mother
saw it, shuddered. We buried it in the backyard
underneath the compost heap. Now my dinner tastes like bones.

The backyard pile of rotted wood we'd pull
apart to see the bugs. We turned a plank into
a table. My friend came to and to the house.
We made a stew of broken rocks. My parents
would not eat the bones (or lick the bones or love the bones).

We knew that there had been a war, and after that
there was a manor; then it all became this town.
Lenape, Wappinger, and butlers thundered through
and through the woods. Sleepless, scared, we'd dig and
listen: shards of them the earth churned up, to us, we thought, to us.

MY MOTHER, TELLING STORIES

Her trowel scraped
bone. My sternum
ached with
little seeds.

She patched the overlayer.
Said, Go down
into the earth,
the only

place I will not follow.
Then rose, skeletal,
from my bed.
I lay

awake in the froglight.
A collection of piano
notes hung
outside.

I rode them.

II

SHORES

THE ROUTE BACK

Here's how to get back to your family, said the water,
*Dive. I'll bring you down to the village, where
your ancestors stand in the trees.* That was how it was
for a while in Seattle. I stood on a bridge
and considered. I was alone. It was hard to resist.

Now I sleep with a book in my head
and the village, Sosenka, inside it. Women
in black skirts with bright eyes: Not heaven.
A place they lived for a while. Shifting between countries
every other war, until there was no one left.

Even the name of the village is dead, filled
with water and drowned: *Sosenka.* The name
wakes in the bedside lamp, here
in Massachusetts, where no one but me
can hear it. Or the house plants discuss

my grandfather's mustache. What kind eyes
he had, sighs the table. Then watches me
climb the steps to my grandmother's house,
although there's no house left. No kindness.
Unsent letter, all of them dead—

Only: once I thought to leave—
I stood on a bridge and waited, my tongue
full of grief. It took nearly too long
for the voices to filter back
talking excitedly of eggs, of fire, of the smell of pulled-up beets.

CAUGHT

Outside, the sea chews
the rocks to salt.

In the room, a crouching
extravagance: spilled silk,
a tumbled glass. The shower hums.
The room contracts.

Whose knuckles are they
that rattle in the glass?
Who jeweled
in the see-through night?

Outside, the sea
chooses carefully—
it does not sink
the city. It does not snuff the sun.

The old cries bead
across the surface of the glass.

 RAVENOUS

A fast turn in the covers and I was pinned
Only then did I realize what I'd let into my bed—

       (hands on my wrists   don't fight it
constriction   and no door
then the sun   rising into the window   cutting me open
me, the husk   *I could force you if I wanted to, you know*
he elaborated   then he let me go)

       I said nothing   later kissed him
walking home   my skin shrank around my hands

SEATTLE

Sometimes I get so wrangled the only thing that calms
me is a deer turning into a tree. Or hands with a ring
on them I can just see through the dark. I manage
a glass of water and a small resurrection of my sister.
Under the ceiling of clouds, we manage occasional
speaking. Our troubled spills. Our restless bowels.
We raise children shaped like clouds who do not notice
out loud. Who manage our silences. Who go on, without asking.

MOTHERLESS

Journey: slept against the grass walls
and dreamed my mother in a bright red dress
chasing me, our feet punctured by bees.

Feet swelled to boats, and at the water
I took ten steps before salt bled
the wounds, the feet deflated, plunging me in—

I sank, hair seaweed, hands webbed,
virginity lost on the silver glint
of a trout's back. Deeper still

in caves, I spoke my old name;
it echoed from the limestone drippings.
In the dark, my eyes reversed.

I could float in this absence, no need
of garage doors, key rings, or plates—

But I looked up at my mother's blue face
above the water. She held palms outward,
eyes fire, then closed against the grass—

I was plunged upward
air scorching my lungs
from where I had stayed without need.

LIVE-IN

The dry attic wood
lapped my feet
as a dog laps water.
I slept on the fifth floor,
above the family,
had a watch and a book.
I did not want to answer
and they would not
make me speak
or be a flower.

Downstairs, the baby
that has just become a girl
runs past me, playing chase.
Her mother points
and I chase her.

Remember

the eyes at the bottom
of each bucket blink
when water is squeezed
from the cloth   and go
when voices call
the children in for dinner
sheep's tail   little fluff
what ails us   in a fishing boat
sliding past the moon

SEE-THROUGH

Light falls off the back of the pond. The pond blurs
and purples, all I need for my arms. Not your small
familiar frame stepping into mine. Instead, years
of trying to be the same color as rocks, water,
anything I walked past,

                   see-through.

A hurt that doesn't give up. Is a stone in me. I feel
my shapes around it.   (Then I forget, I let you
turn the lights on.   Sleuthed out. Solids and yellows.)
I stand at the pond. Concentrate hard on the water.
     When I was young I lay down. Sucked the sun up
from the hot rock.   The beautiful stones.   I pick them up and hold
               them, one after another
thinking *what I'll have when you are gone.*

SEVEN YEARS

since I saw my sister—
I lost the yellow dot of her
folded into the map.
Blinked willingly
and she was gone—

But I don't want to end
with that. I want to end in the yard
under a purple sky, our breath
written on the air,
my sister and I fall back
into waist-high snow . . .

Stars out.
Voices from the house—

SONG IN A BOX

Piano with a house inside
traveled across the country
to be played by my father
at midnight. Note-ghosts
floated up past the sleeping dog

to my room. My father and I
weren't speaking, and the box
my grandmother kept
her hairpins in was more lost
than ever. She was born

in the Third Ward, Newark.
At sixty, began to play
and let nobody hear
but my grandfather. Then
she died, and the sound

was stored in a box only Myer
could find. He died too
and the house was gone,
except in the piano
sometimes though hardly

anyone played. Hear it talking
fadedly of the footshapes
left in her stockings,
those letters we never saw,
of their old whites and blues.

How to Return

The sea is not quite as sad
and then, sometimes, sadder.
Nothing is where she left
it. Her father's voice grown
moss around it. The cousins
have moved. The stairs to their beach
washed away, a space
she tries to reinhabit. The sea
gets another year older, higher,
the waters filling his voice.

Island

She would cry every time we put her in the carriage. That was all right, and the way I had to lean sideways to make her sleep. Her soft breath on my face. Smelled like waste. My back would heal and she would nurse. My nipples still blue when the sound of the ocean stopped. Sometimes the trees bend toward me and I'll feel something like it. Or taste it just before. The gold dripping off the leaves, just before it sweetens and betrays.

III

INTERIORS

LAMB, AFTER FOURTEEN YEARS

First bite, the dining room
came back: mauve tablecloth,
strange fixture—two bulbs
yellowing out of a globe
of chinked translucent tiles—
fireplace, high-backed chairs—and me
still hungry, gnawing flesh
off the bone, discomforting
against my nose,
my mother's gaze—

her face
floated in circles of oil
spreading from the lamb
across the plate. In their walls,
the windows narrowed. My
shoe soles began to fade.
The meat need pulled
at the bottom of my tongue.

A Vacancy

The girl on the highway—don't tell her.
Clock her vacancies in the grandfather
across the hall. Set the eaves by her. Did she forget
the crystal vases, the oak stained dark,
the nothing-ever-breaks-here? We meet
in the highway blackness. She street-grins,
walks backward against the lights. She thinks
she comes from the green mountains *out there*.
But the mantel cries out for her pictures,
her room in a hoarse voice calls her name.
Don't let her hear. Don't trap her. Keep her
from the roaring of mantels, this more than heavy silence of plates.

*

Let's say I was there when the goose bit
her knee and she was carried, crying,
up the hill. Say I was with her when she hurled
a crab across the beach, and I kicked sand
into her eyes. Say we had the same parents,
that she was the golden child, and I was
skinny, runtish, and mean. Say she tried
to get me up a tree, into a cartwheel,
over a chain-link fence, but my body
couldn't—say she tried to rescue me,
unfeeling and cold, only through the eyes
of a sister that never was?

FROM SUMMER'S EMPTY ROOM

From hail's room
from the room drawn on the sail
from the storm room
the captain's room
from the closet
and the closet
within the closet
from the kitchen
the cupboard
the room
where yellow gathers
from the root room
the salt room
the room beneath the house
from the worm room
the dirt room
the room of teeth
and nails

glass slammed to a table
footsteps crunching salt
bootheels on a ladder
clinks against the masts
clap of surf on surf
wood that lifts and bursts

Before Leaving

She found the bird, stuck
between two panes of glass
in the front room as I was
packing up the house.

Not *she* exactly—like
a brother to me.
"I'll take care of it,"
she said, the weight

in the paper bag.
And her look. I chewed
my wrist. "You'll give it
a proper burial," I said.

She put it on the hood
of a BMW.
When I returned,
she'd taken to skirts.

I'd wake in the night,
spitting feathers. Crushed
birds on all sides
of the path. For a while,

finding them, I thought
that the world was speaking.

EVERYTHING'S FERTILE

Everyone's pregnant.
Me, I am growing dogwood blossoms
all over my black shirt.
They bloom, seed, wilt, drop, die.
Out of the seeds
grow eggs and shards of glass,
windows and torn-off doors,
planks and burnt-out arches in one big pile
I am lying under.

IF SHE DRINKS

If she drinks a cup of fire, I dream
a mouth of fire. I find myself absently
caressing her toothbrush. In her room
she pulls dead leaves off the sapling. True,
I was scared. I thought I might be hated,
or smothered in my sleep. But when I woke up
Saturday morning, all the dishes folded
in their cupboards, it felt right
to have another animal moving in the house.

Sometimes I dream there is a third room
we discover, full of permanent furniture.
I reach into the medicine chest and pull out
the half-jaw she keeps there, dry and white.
Then I drink some of her tea. She's in the other
room, writing something down. I break a glass.
The door to her room falls open, the furniture
tells me she is kind and absent, offers
some small pieces I can add to my mouth.

WHEN DAY IS DONE

My parents chose
a house with ghosts.
Where we ripped

up the rugs, we found
phrases scratched
into the floor—and where

the wallpaper had
stripped into hooks.
Red sentences

stuck into sconces
and lit, we ate our dinner.
I folded my hips into

an envelope slipped
under a door.
Sleep

a voice rasped
from the keyhole
and the letters

began to tighten.
So my mother started
singing at my bed—

     Ramona . . . da-da-da-di
da-da-da-daa-da

cutting another hallway
into my heart.

BLUEPRINT

Move into a house where love sleeps
next to you, hiding in a mouth all night
long. Stand on tiptoe on the porch steps,
see yearning placed carefully at the top
of the built-in. Protozoa swim
under the floor. Share kitchen table,
tablecloth, all the whites and colors.
For autumn, go on bathing in this orange
light. For winter, fireplace. The field
or willow trees with snow again. Recent drafts
of houses. Bridge over Alewife Brook. I saw
a great blue heron once and thought of her
somewhere, waiting for a door to step through.
Little kitchen. Brightly colored cloths.
And want to be that doorway.

BLIND AND DELIGHTED

we ate out on the porch the last of summer
nothing was wrong   bugs and the neighborhood made
small noises   we balanced plates on our legs
sausage and eggs   I'd scrambled   she looked at
me said   let's take a walk   I wanted to go
back to bed   so we did   night came   we drove
to a friend's to walk the dog   I cooked   chopped
onions   sliced knife   into my finger   she held
it in the lamplight   said don't look   I watched
her watch the finger   dropped her at the bus   her hair
falls against her face   a way that hurts me
will hurt me later   while part of me   blind and delighted taps
me on the shoulder as I watch her taps   taps me again

WHAT LOST WAS LIKE

Every family in the country eating dinner.
Sixteen, I'd locked myself

permanently out of the house.
Some hard thing

made an edge in me
I pocketed, unable to enter any window.

THE YEAR WITH NO ADDRESS

A train, trees, houses. Where
was I going? Sleeping
in a friend's guest bedroom
with no job and no plan.

Across the aisle, a man leaned
wanting my story. He had
a house in Newton and a nice overcoat.
You're free, he said

meaning *not like me.*
He thought he knew the home
I could go back to, solid foundation
in the sucking earth. That I could afford

mistakes. And I, white
in thrift store skirt, looked the part.
At my friend's house I ranted
as she folded napkins.

She had some ideas about the way
he saw it. Her husband
said nothing, sorting mail
in the background. I could not return

the favor—that was the fault line
in our friendship forever. A strange
feeling in the house: a home,
though I wasn't home; blind

like when you gain
weight suddenly and walk
into things. Soft blue carpet, a two-
car garage: these things can trip

you up. They can put you
right to sleep. Even now
I don't like to think about the time
when I had nowhere to go but her.

VILLAGE AT THE END OF THE OIL ROAD

When I woke at the oil camp, the others
had gone. The camp fenced off the jungle, but not
the heat of extraction. Neat squares of dorms, a gym.
M—, the caretaker, talked with me
on the porch, where dead katydids had fallen
overnight. Un momento, he said, and grabbed one,
ripping off its wings as he ran. ¡Venga! ¡Venga!
he said, and I went. A yellow-green bird hopped
from the porch rail onto his finger. Pepito.
The workers had saved him when he fell
from a light pole. He ate the soft green body
out of M—'s hand. By afternoon, I'd return
to the village, where women took me
to wash clothes in the only clean river. Two days later,
graffiti at the school: *Hello, I am white for whoever*
wants to enter. In the longhouse, T— joked
he'd send his grandson back with me to learn
English. But I don't have a house, I said. ¡No
importa! he answered and his daughter laughed
and her son cried until she pulled him into
the hammock with her. Three times a day
Y— gave me a bowl of stew and yucca.
When I left, I could never find the text
that said in recent years the word for *outsider*
had changed from *cannibal*
to *the one we have to feed so they do not starve.*

GO BACK IN THE HOUSE

where the baby sleeps
fiddling its new word.
Its neck bent
as the spine of the cello
the older daughter carries
on her back. Ask her.

Who's unlucky?
Who lies? Who sings
toward the shape
that disappears
at the nursery door.

CRAFTING

Let us not bruise a single onion. Or throw away a single bite of peach. If you have a home, open it. Take in vegetables and homeless youth. Patch the places where their mother ripped hair from their scalp. Tuck carrot peels back into earth.

Take in this muddy river. Banks rise, then freeze and snow again. Take it in your mouth, the headline: Boy, 15, Charged With Murder. As you are charged with water, charged to clean the muddy bootstains by the door. Not the murder, but the fracture it covers. Make home big enough to fit all of this and vegetables and meat. Kids whose lip prints you must clean from glasses, who thunder up and down the stairs. Who must be made dinner and spoken to with an unfractured voice.

Take the glove that got left in the river. Your own sadness, snap it open in the basement in the yellow lights. The table littered with feathers, bones. Feet shuffle upstairs, stomp, then rest. Your work laid out before you, and almost enough time.

IV

OUT FURTHER

Runaways, Apartment

Here is what we had:
a pair of scissors. A few
dry scraps of paint. CDs
we'd stolen from our parents.
A roll of string. We dumped
our tips on the rug. Counted them
and got groceries. We made red meat
for the man upstairs. August
pulled the smoke to him.
But it was our skin smell
he was stumbling to. We heard
thumping that grew louder, then
groans. There was nothing
that did not make us laugh.
The trees shed petals
compulsively. We dared each other
to put our feet on the grill.

HOLLY, 1962

After Bridget Potter

I thought horizon was made up in stories—even
in the country, New York,
hills and trees zip past the eye up close to the train
I ride home or back
to the city where something terrible would befall me,
I was warned, and perhaps
has: three weeks ago I sat cooking in a scalding bath,
Kevin pouring gin
into my mouth to induce abortion. No luck. Now, three hundred
dollars in my bra,
on a plane to California, I see the earth receding to its side. So that's
horizon. On the ground
it is a sideways spine, crossed by the uneven vertebraeic trees,
the same long line
I trace down the hall, where the tubular bulbs have yellowed
out like bones,
to the room where I lie on my back and listen for the scraping
I am author to.
Weeks of crying at my desk, a douche with soap,
running up and down
the stairs, the bath and gin, a visit to a witch with a folding table
I ran from scared—then
a name in my ear from a friend back home, the frantic push
for money, the flight
and now the pain that tastes like metal, that crests, to stay
Holly, me, *this* Holly.
I feel a pulling all through. Then I am packed with rags and bleeding
in the cab. The sun
and pain conspire, the hotel dark and yellow. I am dumb

with it, all night listening
to it, and for whether it will kill me. At the airport,
the trees become
long necks, their hair fronds dangle far above the ground.
In New York, the world
comes close again. The same music pouring out of the same bars,
the food familiar
as my own body. Someday, at a party, a stranger will describe
your trees, and I affect
indifference as he makes the introduction—
California, me, California:
no one else in this city will know how we met.

ONE MUST GO

My sister went out to sea while I stayed
at home with the dog—the animal warmth of him
solids my hands; he smells of kippers, wet branches, my

sister's body bloody after battle, heaving
on the floor of the ship. I never came to anyone in dreams.
I have one sword leaned against the wall, my sister's,

knocked over repeatedly by the dog. He wheels
and gruffs like when they came to collect her,
four of them, the dead army sound of their knock

shaking the frame. The kettle cracked. One,
they said. And my sister's eyes took shape
as they pointed past me. She stomped, floor shaking,

out the door. A year later, she was queen. The next
she lost a hand, the next an eye. She appeared
to men in dreams, menstrual, huge, to draw them out

further, their ships wracked to splinters, my sister
knocked, shaking, out further than I ever—
windows suck ash against their railings, and I
am on the kitchen floor, my animal hand alive in the dog's fur.

DESAHOGARSE

In Spanish, home, *hogar,* sounds like drown,
                    ahogar, but Laura tells me
there's no relation. At Laura's house,
we leave doors open because we want
to laugh and gather. Laura shares
the big bed with her mother
even when they are not
speaking.   *Desahogarse*
is to unburden yourself, not to undrown
or even to unhome.
                    When I go home

I still don't know how to talk.
                    Casa is house and
                    casarse to marry
and when you marry yourself
with another, you house yourself I think.
In my house,
any closed door was opened,
so I could not be naked.

In the catalog of dreams about my mother,
there's one where I search for keys
in her white apartment, a place
she's never lived. I'm leaving,
                    unhoming myself
without drowning.
                    When I go back
to the house, it's different: I still don't know

what to do with the voices in the attic.

                    But downstairs,

outside,

in the huge lights the windows throw across the dark,

a deer bucks and leaps

in the driveway.

                    And I can stand there

                    watch it dancing.

GOING TO PALMYRA

Bouquets of cut branches   fruit-heavy on the dusty street
Pink fish scales' arc   from knife to air   Pastaza   Amazon city:
nothing behind glass   everything close   Through the bus window
a woman hands me a baby   When he cries   she pulls him down
hands me a sack   We are going to Palmyra   market by the Napo
where the oil-ravaged   sell endangered birds   where men bought rifles
to kill the family hiding from the oil roads   I heard
they used guns   because they are no longer strong enough
to hold spears   In this story   I am always white   always American
never know what's true   When we arrive   the beer is gone
women sell toys and clothes   Food carts close for the afternoon
Waorani cross back to Block 16 in metal canoes
I walk out of the market   up the dirt road   past leaves big as my torso
to the monjitas' museum   Cool air in their cement building
On display: The nine-foot spears that killed
missionaries bringing Christ and oil   that scared away tree-strippers
in the rubber boom   On the sanctuary floor   a spiral of leaves and stones
She says   we made it to understand the indigenous life
Here is water   here is soil   and here la comunidad
Alone   the forest kills you   but with the others   you are safe
Back at the market   children throw achiote shells   at the metal shed roof
that makes a square of shade   in the cleared stretch
D— laughs at my sunburnt face   We ride back to Pastaza
where his body clenches   at the blaring music
I write down everything he says   I don't know what good
he thinks that this will do   but I believe
in my power   to do good   the essay
once published will change nothing   I will still
want to be here always   That's a lie   I will always want to have been here

V

WAYS IN THE DARK

LION

I knew, you knew
the lion was out.
We slept the side
of the mountain.
The lion waited.
I began to steepen,
slip. Above
you built a fire.
Up above on a ledge
of rock. Smart, I thought.
That would keep the lion
back. But I was slip-
ping down. I heard
his, his ocher.
Saw him pace
the side. Now I wrestle,
pull the hot skin of him
from the muscle.
We slide with rocks
and gravel. In the tent
you sleep and wait.
I wrestle. I want to stop,
to climb and wake
you, to tell you that
it's time now
but it isn't time.

Tonight, Under the Blanket

What about the body
                of a child
fern-shaped and fitted
to your side?
It is split off—
        My father walks
through the haunted woods
the small worry
        that was my body
safe on his back   under the blanket
        And tonight   when all
I want is to be carried
I feel my body split off
from the bed   no
body
        against mine   no body
forgetting its borders in the dark
as though the moment
I was set down at the edge
of the woods   I stumbled
        forward on new legs
toward what
        I had forgotten
toward this

SUMMER

We hated to be photographed.
Photograph is a lie of seeing
but also it made us dead.
Invented strange rebellions.
Lied as if by accident.
In all that time of opening,
I was never touched. Except by leaves.
By the bird flying too close
over my head. Except on the old gray
mattress, too young to know
to reach for her. Still.

Kahee and the Dark

North of Xi'an, I'd wake
unable to find my hands.

She and I went for oranges.
We held them, sweet and tart, the only bright things
in the sudden fog.

Husks burned
at the edges of the fields.
We walked home without our feet.

Later, the notes of her flute drifted down the hall.
It spoke of a forest.
How you sing when you walk, not to lose yourself.

The song stopped and the dark
erased the room.

TUNNEL

The outer world: tree blocked all sight.
First, I saw one wing remove itself by
light. Then, the falcon. Shadowed
by the tunnel of leaves as it flew,
in its beak, the iridescent wing of the pigeon.

It's terrible: your mouth on
my neck in the orange-glow. My
skin wakes to you, and wants. Even
as you pull yourself backward through
the bed, the iridescent *with* in your mouth.

TRANSITION

If you had another body,
maybe a stag—but the deer

had to be a boy now, had to take
a boy's ways and gestures.

Childish to insist on a story,
not the body, not the parts

of you I don't know.
When you enter me, my hooves

trample the floorboards,
the skeleton of a hoop skirt

goes up in flame—
the invisible in me

wrestling itself towards form.

MY THEOLOGY

My body was trying
to get itself back
into the silver-white
bucking through the woods—
before skin, pink
nipples, patch
of matted black hair,
back into the wild
thing with one sharp horn—
while under you, the body
you were holding
(the real thing, whatever that was)
groaned and rose.

EARTHWORK

For Ruth

She loves me now, more now
since I've been branded—

comes back to me, hands only,
tunneling through the dirt,

thick with rings. She is trying
to tell me through the roar—

how flowers tunnel under
to be pummeled

how the skin shudders
just before it breaks away.

AYIL

And one day—
    the tree reveals
its blue-green flame

you see the antlers at the center
        have raised themselves
to your very face

you go on
    from there   the animal
at your side

NOTES

The title of "From Summer's Empty Room" is taken from Emily Dickinson's poem 291, "It sifts from Leaden Sieves."

Sosenka, the village mentioned in "Returning," was located in the Vilna Gubierna of Russia, and is now in Belarus.

"Holly, 1962" is a response/interpretation of the essay "Lucky Girl," by Bridget Potter.

Some of the poems in this book are true, and some just feel true, but the poems about the rainforest are as accurate as my memory, notes, and sources allow. "Reporting From Block 16" refers to the part of the Ecuadoran Amazon where the oil company Repsol operates. It is also part of the territory of the Waorani people, who lived in voluntary isolation until the 1950s, when American missionaries, helped along by oil companies, doggedly pursued contact.

An oil road runs over 100 kilometers south into Block 16, starting at the Napo River. Both "Reporting From Block 16" and "Village at the End of the Oil Road" take place near what used to be the end of this road (it has since expanded). The word for "outsider" in Wao Terero, the Waorani language, is "cowodi."

The Palmyra Market in "Going to Palmyra" is just outside Block 16, on the northern banks of the Napo River, across from Repsol's gates.

In Hebrew, the word transliterated as "ayil" means both oak tree and stag.

Acknowledgments

Grateful acknowledgment to the editors of the publications in which these poems have appeared, some of them in slightly different form:

Beltway Poetry Quarterly, "Dawn"

Clarion, "In Wolf Country," "My Mother, Telling Stories"

Colorado Review, "Desahogarse"

Contrary, "Lamb, After Fourteen Years," "If She Drinks"

Copper Nickel, "The Year With No Address," "Village at the
      End of the Oil Road"

Denver Quarterly, "Lion," "Island," "Before Leaving"

Green Mountains Review, "Summer," "Kahee and the Dark"

Harbor Review, "Holly, 1962"

Harvard Review, "What We Kept"

La Fovea, "A Vacancy," "Runaways, Apartment"

Pebble Lake Review, "See-Through"

Quarterly West, "Go Back in the House," "Caught"

Sixth Finch, "Blueprint"

*Stoked Words: An Anthology of Poetry from the Capturing Fire Slam and
      Summit,* "My Aunt, the Artist, the Liar"

The Los Angeles Review, "Crafting" (as winner of the Orlando Prize)

The Moth, "The Route Back"

This book came to be in many places: the libraries and coffee shops of Seattle; the top floor of the Richard Hugo House; a month-long residency at Vermont Studio Center made possible by a partial fellowship and generous friends who helped me pay for the rest before crowd-funding was a common thing; rented rooms in the Boston suburbs; a house in West Virginia surrounded by deer that Leigh and Aeolean Jackson generously lent me for a weekend; the firefly-covered hills of Bennington, Vermont; an apartment in Quito, Ecuador, where I started writing poems again after a two-year hiatus; the floor of a living room in Washington, DC, where a friend's cat trampled the pages laid across the floor; and in Marquette, Michigan, at a residency made possible by the Marquette City Chamber. Final edits were completed at a residency at The Studios at MASS MoCA, funded by Assets for Artists. Thank you to all these people, institutions, and places.

All that while, there's been a chorus of voices behind me, an ever-expanding writer family pushing me to continue to transform, and helping me to make the poems better—these poems in particular, and all poems generally. Including, but not limited to (in chronological order): Wang Ping, E. Ethelbert Miller, April Bernard, Timothy Liu, Forrest Gander, Susan Mitchell, Mike Young, Kevin McLellan, Rob MacDonald, Kelli Newby, Sarah Blake, Regie Cabico, Danielle Evannou, Sarah Ann Winn, Randon Noble, Natalie Illum, Janeen

Pergrin Rastall, Marty Achatz, and Jakob Van Lammeran. Thank you for teaching me, supporting me, and making me better. I'm also grateful for the support of Wendy Call, Lara Jakes, Elizabeth Cox, Shaindel Beers, Jennifer Givhan, Ellen Graf, and the Binder Poets.

Thanks also go to Sparkle DC and The Inner Loop, and the incredible writers behind those communities (Regie and Danielle; Rachel Coonce and Courtney Sexton). Thank you to A Room of Her Own Foundation for the Orlando Prize, and Virginia Center for the Creative Arts for a much-needed residency. Thanks to the *Harbor Review* for the surprise and honor of a Best of the Net nomination.

A thank you is utterly inadequate to the Waorani people for speaking to me, taking me into their houses, and showing me the forest. Their defense of their territory is a defense of all beings, of the very air we breathe.

Thanks to my dad for saying "this is your story."

Huge thanks to the editors at Airlie Press for giving this book life, and for their support along the way. Thank you to Airlie's book designer, Beth C. Ford, for her talent, patience, and beautiful illustrations, and to Sara Everett for the use of her haunting painting.

Thanks to the ancestors. Thanks to the voices.

ABOUT THE PUBLISHER

Airlie Press is run by writers. A nonprofit publishing collective, the press is dedicated to producing beautiful and compelling books of poetry. Its mission is to offer a shared-work publishing alternative for writers working in the Pacific Northwest. Airlie Press is supported by book sales, grants, and donations. All funds return to the press for the creation of new books of poetry.

COLOPHON

The poems are set in Adobe Caslon Pro. For the Caslon revival, designer Carol Twombly studied specimen pages printed by William Caslon between 1734 and 1770. The poem titles are in Trajan Pro. The book titles are in the sans serif Tall Films from GemFonts. Printed in Portland, Oregon, USA.